by Dorothy Spangler

Orlando Austin New York San Diego Toronto London

Visit *The Learning Site!*
www.harcourtschool.com

Introduction

Stand outside on a sunny day. Find your shadow.

What does your shadow look like? Is it all near your feet? Or does it stretch far away from you?

Your shadow does not look the same all day. Around noon, your shadow is short. In the early morning or late afternoon, it looks very long. Your shadow changes as the time of day changes.

Today we have clocks and watches to measure time. Long ago, people did not have these things. They measured time in other ways. One way was with shadows. They made timepieces called sundials.

A sundial has two main parts. The first part is a face marked with the hours. The second part is a pointer. The pointer casts a shadow on the face of the sundial.

How a Sundial Works

A sundial needs sunlight to work. On a sunny day, the pointer on the sundial makes a shadow. The shadow falls on the sundial's marked face. The mark tells what the time is.

To tell the time, the pointer must point north. The pointer also must tilt to get the most direct sunlight.

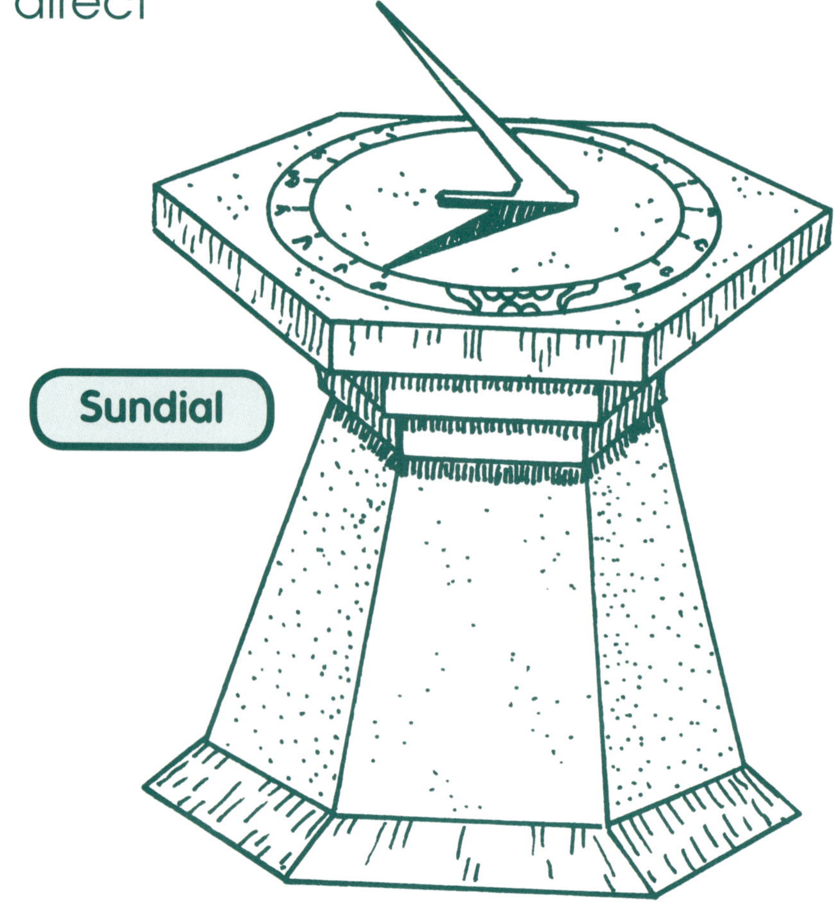

Sundial Time

A sundial measures solar time. Solar means "of the sun."

Solar time is not always the same as clock time. The number of minutes in a clock hour does not change. Each hour on a clock is 60 minutes long.

Solar time is different. A solar hour has no minutes. There are always 12 solar hours between sunrise and sunset. However, the hours are longer in the summer than in the winter.

◀ **Solar Time**
This sundial is showing five o'clock "solar time."

Early Sundials

Who made the first sundials?

Long ago in Egypt, people built tall thin towers. Like the pointer on a sundial, the tower cast a shadow. The shadow showed when it was morning and when it was afternoon.

The Egyptians made the first sundials with round, flat faces. Later, Greeks and Romans made sundials in many shapes and sizes.

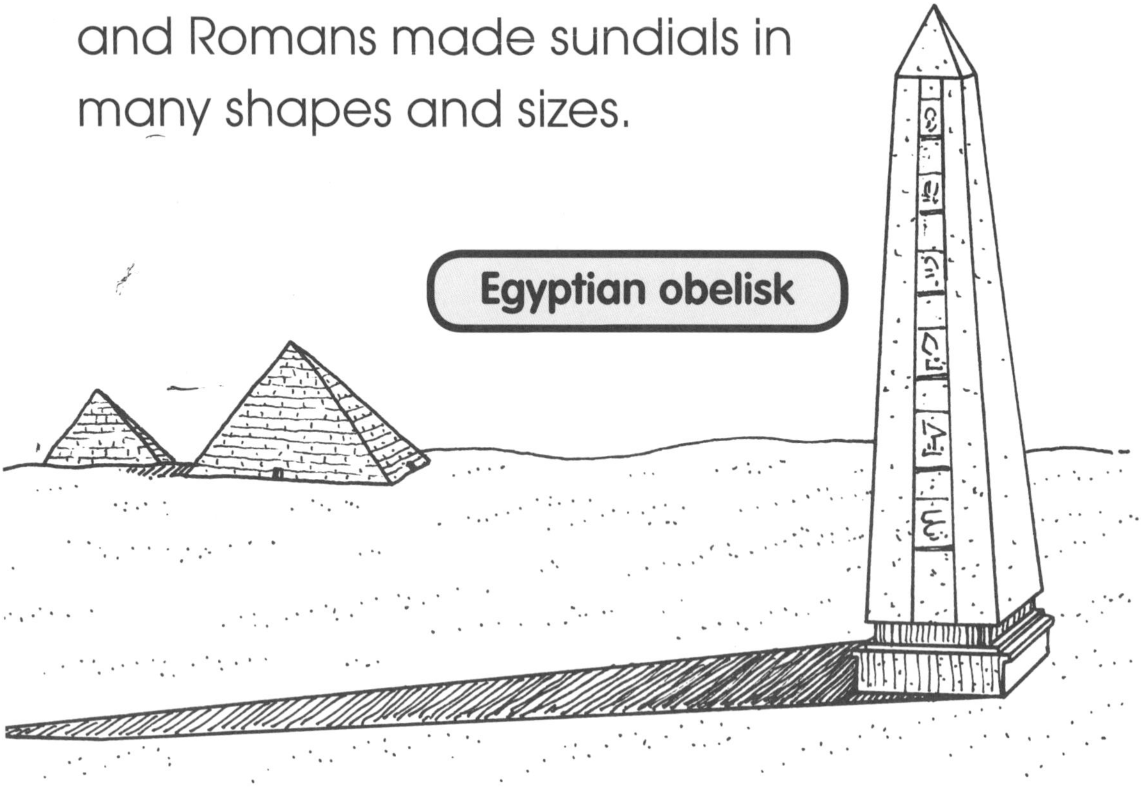

Egyptian obelisk

The Greeks made sundials shaped like bowls. The hour marks were in the hollow of the bowl.

Some Romans had sundials that were very small. They carried these sundials in their pockets. Sort of like a watch!

The early Chinese also made sundials. Their sundials measured the lengths of shadows.

Sundials Today

You can still see sundials in many places. Some people put them in their gardens. Sundials can be found beside buildings and in parks.

A sundial works anywhere the sun shines. There is a sundial on the planet Mars! It was carried there by the *Mars Surveyor* Lander in 2002.

Mars Sundial